A SIXTEENTH-CENTURY

ANTHEM BOOK

Compiled by
CHRISTOPHER MORRIS

FIFTH EDITION (REVISED)

Music Department
OXFORD UNIVERSITY PRESS
LONDON · NEW YORK · TORONTO

OXFORD UNIVERSITY PRESS
Music Department, 37 Dover Street, London W1X 4AH

First Edition 1960
Second Edition (Revised) 1967
Third Edition (Revised) 1969
Fourth Edition (Revised) 1973
Fifth Edition (Revised) 1976

© 1976 by Oxford University Press

Reproduced and printed by
Halstan & Co. Ltd., Amersham, Bucks., England

Publisher's Note

Some of the music in this book was actually composed in the early seventeenth century. But all of it belongs to the sixteenth-century idiom and each of the composers represented lived in that century.

Since the collection is restricted to anthems written for four voices, some well-known names of the period have been omitted. Other prominent composers such as Orlando Gibbons are already represented by four-part anthems in *The Church Anthem Book* (Oxford University Press). Where this is so it was decided that duplication between the two books was undesirable.

The main seasons and festivals of the Church's Year are covered, with the exception of Christmas. At this season the anthem is often replaced by carols, and it was therefore thought more useful to include some anthems for general use.

Thanks are due to the Rev. W. M. Atkins F.S.A. for his valuable advice.

Second Edition
Revised editions of numbers 1, 2, and 3 were added at the back of the book.

Third Edition
Revised editions of numbers 1, 2, and 3 replaced the original editions. Revised editions of numbers 10 and 20 were added at the back of the book.

Fourth Edition
Revised editions of numbers 10 and 20 replaced the original editions. Revised editions of numbers 4 and 8 were added at the back of the book.

Fifth Edition
Revised editions of numbers 4, 8, and 12 have now replaced the original editions.

Alphabetical Index

Index of Composers

Index of Anthems
Suitable for Various Seasons and Occasions

1. REJOICE IN THE LORD ALWAY

Edited by E. H. FELLOWES
Revised edition by PETER LE HURAY
and DAVID WILLCOCKS

ANON. (16th c.)

Philippians IV, 4-7

Source: The only known text of this anthem is the *Mulliner Book*, B.M. Add. MS 30513, in which the music is written in short score and without any words. The words of the Authorised version of the Bible have been added to the MS in a much later hand, but the rhythm of the music makes it clear that the original text must have been that printed in the 1549 Prayer Book as the Epistle for the 4th Sunday in Advent. This text has accordingly been used in the present edition. The original keyboard reduction is printed exactly as it stands in Add. MS 30513 (see the organ part). Some slight rhythmic modifications have been made to the adapted vocal parts. Barring, small notes, small accidentals, monitory accidentals in round brackets, ties crossed through thus ‒‖‒, and all dynamic markings are editorial. The underlay is editorial, and spelling has been modernised. The anthem was once thought to have been composed by John Redford.

No.1. Anon. (16th c.): Rejoice in the Lord alway

No.1. Anon. (16th c.): Rejoice in the Lord alway

2. AUDIVI, MEDIA NOCTE

Edited by R.R.TERRY
Revised edition by PETER LE HURAY
and DAVID WILLCOCKS

THOMAS TALLIS

Editorial Commentary: Small notes, small accidentals, text in square brackets, slurs, and bar-lines are editorial. Bar-lines have no accentual significance. In many places in the original the Latin text is not given in full but is indicated by the use of repeat marks (·/·); in such places the printed text has been italicised. Spelling has been modernised. **Source:** British Museum, Add. MSS 17802-5: i, 17803; ii, 17802; iii, 17804; iv, 17805 (numbering downwards).
Text: The 8th. Respond at Matins on All Saints' Day.
The chant upon which Tallis based his work is to be found in the *Antiphonale Sarisburiense*, fasc. XIX and XX, 567 (Plainsong and Medieval Music Society, 1911). The central section of the Sarum chant (see Figs. A to B) should be inserted after bar 15, and again (Figs. C to B) after bar 49. **Variant:** 14.i.l.: '-vi,' not 15.i.l.

*see editorial note

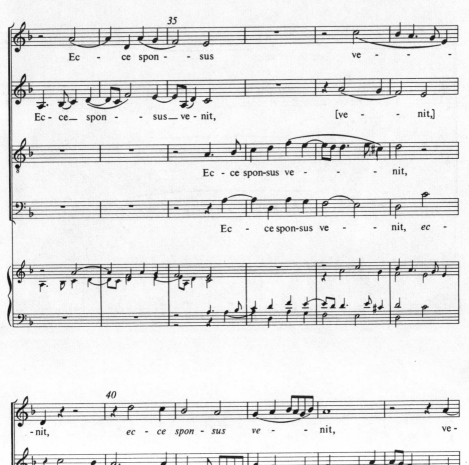

3. NOLO MORTEM PECCATORIS

Edited by Sylvia Townsend Warner
Revised edition by John Morehen

THOMAS MORLEY

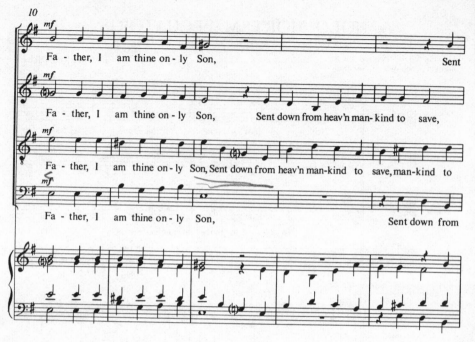

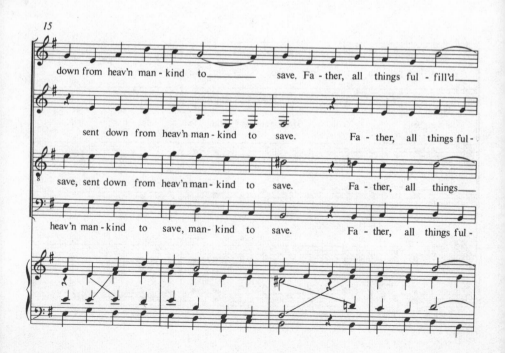

Fa - ther, be - hold my pain - ful smart,   Ta -

Fa - ther, be - hold my pain - ful smart,   Ta - ken for

Fa - ther, be - hold my pain - ful smart,

Fa - ther, be - hold my pain - ful

-ken for man on ev' - ry side;   Ev'n from my birth

man on ev' - ry side, on ev' - ry side;   Ev'n from my birth to

Ta - ken for man on ev' - ry side;   Ev'n

smart, Ta - ken for man on ev' - ry side;   Ev'n

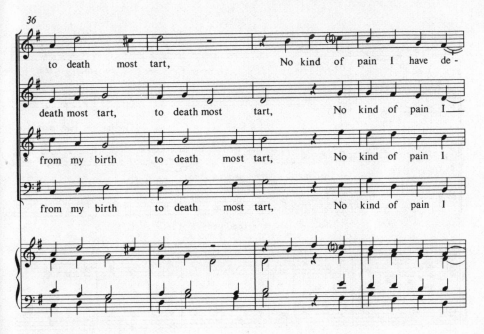

EDITORIAL NOTE

SOURCES

The only source of this secular motet is British Museum, Additional MSS. 29372–5. This important set of secular part-books is in the hand of Thomas Myriell of Chichester and is dated 1616; the anthology is entitled *Tristitiae Remedium*. The four part-books (from the complete set of six) which contain this piece are the Cantus, Altus, Tenor and Bassus books; despite the rather unusual range of the inner parts there is no reason to believe that the motet was originally intended to be sung by men's voices.

While working in Washington D.C. in the Spring of 1966 the revising editor chanced upon what is believed to be the only complete version of the text of the medieval carol from which Morley selected his text for 'Nolo mortem peccatoris.' The source in question, Folger Shakespeare Library, MS. L.b. 562, comprises a single folio sheet and is datable *c*. 1570. There appear to be no printed references to this important document, which belongs to the collection of Loseley papers purchased by the Folger Library in 1954. The manuscript is endorsed in the hand of Sir William More (1520–1600) as follows: 'Two dittyes given me by my L.[ord] Montagu.'[1] It shows that the song originally consisted of twenty-three sextains, and not the four quatrains found in the earlier—but widely differing—version in St. John's College, Cambridge, MS. 259 (late fifteenth century)[2]; in all the versions each stanza concludes with the cauda *Nolo mortem peccatoris*. The first two stanzas as found in the Folger manuscript differ only slightly from those used by Morley, and they are given here with variants from Morley's text printed in italic type.

> Father, I am thine only Son,
>   Sent down from heaven mankind to save.
> Father, all things fulfilled and done
>   According to thy will, I have.
> Father, *now all my will* is this:
>   Nolo mortem peccatoris.
>
> Father, behold my painful smart,
>   Taken for man on every side;
> Even from my birth to death most tart,
>   No kind of *pains* I have denied,
> But suffered all *for love of this:*
>   Nolo mortem peccatoris.

EDITORIAL METHOD

'Cancelling' accidentals are engraved small and redundant accidentals are omitted; accidentals in round brackets are cautionary and not optional. The keyboard reduction, the crossed slurs and the expression marks are all editorial. The spelling and punctuation have been modernized.

ACKNOWLEDGEMENTS

Grateful acknowledgement is made to the governing bodies of the libraries concerned.

J.M.

---

[1] Montagu, Anthony Browne, 1st Viscount (*c*. 1528–1592). The other 'ditty' is found in the related Folger Library manuscript L.b. 563, which like L.b. 562 comprises a single folio sheet; the two manuscripts bear identical watermarks and were probably copied at the same time. The poem in MS. L.b. 563 is entitled 'If gifts of grace in all times past'; it consists of eleven seven-line stanzas and takes the form of verses addressed by our Lord to sinful man.

[2] Folio 9. See Carleton Browne and Rossell Hope Robbins, *The Index of Middle English Verse* (New York, 1943), p. 124. The complete text of the St. John's College version is given by M. R. James and G. C. Macaulay in 'Fifteenth-Century Carols and other Pieces', in *Modern Language Review*, Volume VIII (1913), pp. 79–80.

4. LORD, WE BESEECH THEE

Edited by Percy C. Buck
Revised edition by John Morehen

ADRIAN BATTEN

For Editorial Note see page 98

1) There is verbal confusion here in the 1641 publication.

2) Crotchet (as reduced) in Barnard's *First Book*.

5. LET MY COMPLAINT COME BEFORE THEE

Ps. 119, vv. 169–172, 175

ADRIAN BATTEN
(Ed. MAURICE BEVAN)

Sources: Gostling Part Books, York. St. Paul's Cathedral Part Books (17th cent. Tenor and Bass only)
Note values have been halved, and the anthem has been transposed up one tone.

© 1960, Oxford University Press

* The sharp is clearly marked in the Medius Decani part book.

6. BENEDICTUS QUI VENIT

(BLESSED IS HE THAT COMETH)

PALESTRINA
(Ed. BERNARD ROSE)

From *Missa Quarta* (1582)
© 1957, Oxford University Press

7. THIS IS THE DAY

(EASTER GRADUAL)

Ps. 118, v. 24

Anon.(c. 1600)
(Ed. MAURICE BEVAN)

Canon at the octave below between S&T, A&B, Canon at the Fifth above between S&A, T&B.
Sources: Peterhouse MSS. 42-4, 35-6.
Note values are halved, barlines are added and the piece has been transposed up a minor third.

© 1960, Oxford University Press

* This note is omitted in error in the MS.

8. WHEN THE LORD TURNED AGAIN

Edited by Percy C. Buck
Revised edition by John Morehen

ADRIAN BATTEN

For Editorial Note see page 98

9. LIFT UP YOUR HEADS O YE GATES

Ps. 24, vv. 7, 8a, 10b

JOHN AMNER
(Ed. MAURICE BEVAN)

Note values are halved, barlines are added, and the anthem is transposed up one tone.
Sources : Peterhouse MSS 33, 34, 34a, 39.
*The whole of the Tenor part is missing, and the Bass part is missing at the words 'Who is the King of Glory?' These have been reconstructed by the editor.

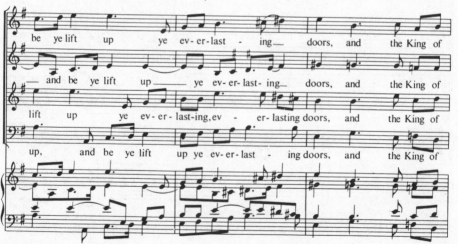

* See note on first page.

10. O LORD, GIVE THY HOLY SPIRIT

Edited by A. RAMSBOTHAM
Revised edition by ANTHONY GREENING

THOMAS TALLIS

* Pronounced as one syllable

days of   our   life: that we may   know   thee, the on-ly true   God,   and

days of_ our_   life: that   we may know   thee, the on-ly   true   God,

days of_ our_   life: that   we may know   thee,   the on-ly true

days of our   life: that   we may know   thee, the on-ly   true   God,

Je-sus Christ whom thou   hast   sent, and Je-sus Christ   whom thou_ hast_ sent, and

and Je-sus Christ whom_ thou   hast sent,   and Je-sus Christ whom thou hast_____ sent,

God,   and   Je-sus Christ whom thou hast sent,   and Je-sus Christ whom thou hast_ sent, and

and Je-sus Christ whom thou hast   sent,   and Je-sus Christ whom thou hast   sent, and

1. Sources:

A   British Museum: (1) Add. Ms. 15166   c. 1567
                    (2) Add. Ms. 29289   c. 1625
                    (3) Add. Ms. 30478   c. 1640
B   St. Michael's College, Tenbury: Ms. 1382   1617
C   New York Public Library: Drexel Mss. 4180—3
                                          c. 1625
D   Gloucester Cathedral Library: Mss. 95 & 96
                                          c. 1641
E   Barnard's 'First Book of Selected Church Music'
                                          1641
F   Ely Cathedral: Mss. 4 & 28   c. 1670
G   York Minster Library: The Decani books of the
    'Gostling' set   c. 1675
H   British Museum: Harl Ms. 7337   c. 1715

2. Editorial Practice:
Small notes, small accidentals, cautionary accidentals
in brackets, small rests, and crossed slurs are editorial.

3. Variants:

The tenor part has a key signature of a single B flat in
sources A(3), C, D & G.

Source	/	bar	/	stave	/	beat	/	variant
Ely Ms 4	/	1	/	6	/	1-4	/	semibreve B flat
A(1), C & G	/	2-3	/	1	/	3-4-1	/	crotchet B flat minim B flat
Ely Ms 4	/	9	/	5	/	2	/	natural to A
Ely Ms 4	/	14	/	5	/	3-4	/	minim G flat
G		/ 14-15	/	1	/	4-1-2	/	minim F, crotchet F
H		/	17	/	2	/	2½	/	semiquavers F, [G flat
A(3), E & F	/	19	/	repeat bar missing				
C		/	20	/	4	/	3-4	/	natural to A
A(1)		/	21	/	1	/	3	/	rest missing

II. HOLY, HOLY, HOLY

PALESTRINA
(Ed. BERNARD ROSE)

From *Missa Quarta* (1582)

© 1957, Oxford University Press

*There is no Amen in the original Latin setting. This Amen is taken from the *Creed*. Ed.

12. SACERDOTES DOMINI

(Then did priests make offering)

Edited by R. R. TERRY
Revised edition by JOHN MOREHEN

WILLIAM BYRD

★ For Editorial Note see page 98

13. SING UNTO THE LORD

Ps. 30, vv. 4, 11–13

CHRISTOPHER TYE
(Ed. A. RAMSBOTHAM)

From *I will Exalt Thee*
© 1936, Oxford University Press

14. OF THE GLORIOUS BODY TELLING

(GENITORI GENITOQUE)

St. Thomas Aquinas, Hymn for Vespers of Corpus Christi

T. L. de VICTORIA

From *De Corpore Christi (More Hispano)*

15. O SING JOYFULLY

Ps. 81, vv. 1–4

ADRIAN BATTEN
(Ed. MAURICE BEVAN)

Source: York, Gostling part-books (Decani set)

© 1960, Oxford University Press

*Original underlay of words.

Note values have been halved, bar-lines have been added and the anthem has been transposed up a minor third.
Note: In a previous edition, this anthem appeared under the title 'Sing we merrily unto God'. The words are restored in this present edition to their original form to avoid confusion with Batten's anthem 'Sing we merrily' for seven voices, which appears in R.C.M. MSS 1045-51.

16. EXSULTATE JUSTI

(*PRAISE YOUR GOD, YE RIGHTEOUS*)

Ps. 32, vv. 1–3 (Vulgate)

English translation
by B. R.

LUDOVICO VIADANA
(Ed. BERNARR RAINBOW)

Source: BM F278 vol I.6. f20.
If an organ is used it is suggested that during the bracketed passages the voices are unaccompanied

senza pedale

legato

— ye a new_____ song.
- ti-cum no - - - - - - - - - - vum,

ye a new_____ song. O sing be - ne
- - ti - cum no - - - - - vum, be - ne

— ye, sing, sing ye. O sing
- - ti - cum no - vum, be - ne

ye a new_____ song.
- - ti - cum no - - - - - vum.

O sing prai - ses, sing prai - ses: sing lu - sti - ly with good
be - ne psal - li - te e - - i in vo - ci - fe - ra - ti -

prai - ses, sing prai - ses, O sing prai - ses, sing prai - ses: sing lu - sti - ly with
psal - li - te e - i, be - ne psal - li - te e i in vo - ci - fe - ra -

prai - ses, sing prai - ses: sing lu - - sti - ly_____ with good
psal - li - te e - - i in vo - - ci - fe - - - ra - ti -

with _____ good cour - - - - - - - - - age.
-ra - - - - - - -ti - o - - - - - - - - - ne.

with good cour - - age, sing lu - sti - ly with good cour - - age.
-ra - ti - o - ne, in vo - ci-fe-ra-ti-o - - ne.

-age, sing lu - - sti - ly with good cour - - age.
-ne, in vo - - ci - fe - ra - ti - o - - ne.

_____ good cour - - - - - - - - - - - age.
- - - - -ti - o - - - - - - - - - - - ne.

Maestoso

Praise your God, ye righ - teous, re - joice and
Ex - sul - ta - te ju - sti in Do - - - mi - -

Praise your God, ye righ - teous, re - joice and
Ex - sul - ta - te ju - sti in Do - - mi - -

Praise your God, ye righ - teous, re - joice and
Ex - sul - ta - te ju - sti in Do - - mi - -

Praise your God, ye righ - teous, re - joice and
Ex - sul - ta - te ju - sti in Do - - mi - -

Maestoso

col. 8va

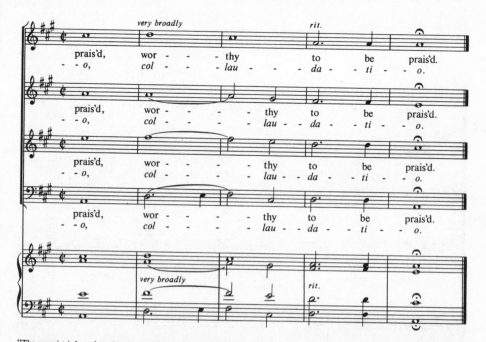

"The organist is bound to play the organ part simply, and in particular with the left hand; if however he wants to execute some movement with the right hand, as by ornamenting the cadences, or by some appropriate embellishment, he must play in such a manner that the singer or singers are not covered or confused by too much movement..... When passages in full harmony are played on the organ, they are to be played with hands and feet......The organ part is never under any obligation to avoid two fifths or two octaves as those parts which are sung by the voices are."
Viadana: Preface to Cento concerti ecclesiastici [1602]

17. O LORD, THE MAKER OF ALL THING

King's Primer, 1545

Anon. (c. 1548)
(Ed. E.H. FELLOWES)

Edited from the "Wanley" MSS c.1548 (Bodl. Mus. Sch. e 420-2) and missing soprano part added.

© 1935, Oxford University Press

Let nei-ther us de-lu--ded be, Good Lord, with dream or fan-ta-sy;

Let nei-ther us de-lu-ded be, Good Lord, with dream or fan-ta-sy;

Let nei-ther us de-lu-ded be, Good Lord, with dream or fan-ta-sy;

Let nei-ther us de-lu-ded be, Good Lord, with dream or fan-ta-sy;

Our hearts wak-ing in thee thou keep That we in sin fall not on sleep,

Our hearts wak-ing in thee thou keep That we in sin fall not on sleep,

Our hearts wak-ing in thee thou keep That we in sin fall not on sleep,

Our hearts wak-ing in thee thou keep

That we in sin fall not on sleep. O Fa-ther, through thy bless--ed Son,

That we in sin fall not on sleep. O Fa-ther, through thy bless-ed Son,

That we in sin fall not on sleep. O Fa-ther, through thy bless-ed Son,

That we in sin fall not on sleep. O Fa-ther, through thy bless-ed Son,

Grant us this our pe - ti - ti - on,   To whom with the Ho - ly Ghost al - ways

Grant us this our pe - ti - ti - on,   To whom with the Ho - ly Ghost al - ways

Grant us this our pe - ti - ti - on,   To whom with the Ho - ly Ghost al - ways

Grant us this our pe - ti - ti - on,   To whom with the Ho - ly Ghost al - ways

In heaven and   earth be laud and praise, In heaven and earth be laud   and praise.

In heaven and earth be laud   and praise, In heaven and earth be laud and   praise.

In heaven and earth be laud and   praise, In heaven and   earth be laud and praise.

In heaven and earth be laud and   praise.

18. O GOD, BE MERCIFUL

Ps. 67, v. 1

CHRISTOPHER TYE
(Ed. P.C. BUCK)

* This Anthem is originally in three parts, the first section ending at this point. The 'So be it' which follows is the Coda to the third section, which itself ends (like the first) on the chord of the dominant.

19. DELIVER US, O LORD OUR GOD

Ps. 106, vv. 45 & 46

ADRIAN BATTEN
(Ed. E. H. FELLOWES)

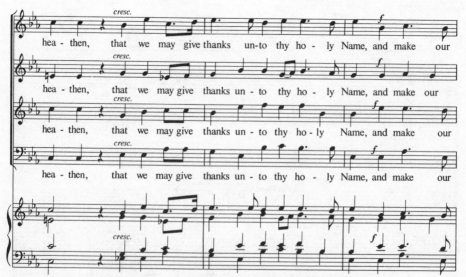

Original: a minor third lower

*The omission of a ♮ here in the early texts is, in the Editor's opinion, an oversight.

© 1929, Oxford University Press.

20. O PRAY FOR THE PEACE OF JERUSALEM

Edited by A. RAMSBOTHAM
Revised edition by ANTHONY GREENING

THOMAS TOMKINS

Text: Ps. 122, v. 6

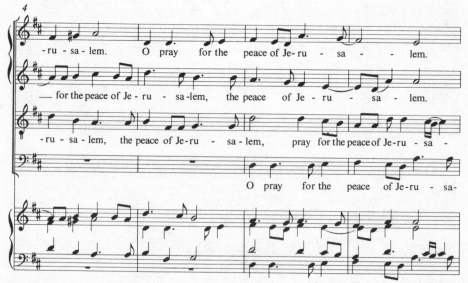

Sources:
A. *Musica Deo Sacra*. 1668 (complete set of part-books)
B. St. John's College, Oxford: Ms. 181, c. 1630. (bass part-book)
C. Royal College of Music: Ms. 1051, c. 1625 (bass part-book)

Editorial Practice:
Small accidentals, small notes, small rests, and cautionary accidentals in brackets are editorial.

* Source B has a pause mark over the final note.

ADRIAN BATTEN
Lord, we beseech thee *and* When the Lord turned again

These revised editions of two of Adrian Batten's best-known compositions are based almost exclusively on the text printed in John Barnard's *First Book of Selected Church Musick* (1641). Both anthems also survive in variant versions in an incomplete set of manuscript part-books assembled (and possibly even copied in part) by John Barnard between approximately 1625 and 1638 (Royal College of Music, MSS. 1045–1051). Adrian Batten and John Barnard were both closely associated with St. Paul's Cathedral during the immediate pre-Civil War period, Batten as a Vicar-Choral and Barnard as a Minor Canon. The present editor is of the opinion that the text of these two anthems published in Barnard's *First Book* represents the composer's own revision for publication of the text found in the 'Barnard manuscripts'. The 1641 printed text has therefore been accorded primacy for this revision, although Barnard's manuscript versions have been consulted for clarification of the printed text in those instances where the latter is open to more than one interpretation.

Accidentals in small type, dynamic markings, the alternative verbal text in square brackets, and the organ parts are editorial. Verbal underlay which still remains speculative after reference to Barnard's manuscript collection is indicated by italic type. Cautionary accidentals are shown in round brackets only when they are not indicated in the original source. Redundant accidentals in the original are tacitly ignored.

J.M.

WILLIAM BYRD
Sacerdotes Domini

Source: *Gradualia*, I, 1605 (York Minster Library). The 1610 reissue (Christ Church Library, Oxford) has also been consulted. The performance directions, the English text, and the keyboard reduction are by R. R. Terry. The original clefs are as follows:

(Superius)   (Medius)   (Tenor)   (Bassus)

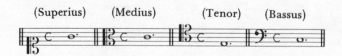

Small accidentals and cautionary accidentals in brackets are editorial. The sign ⌐‾‾‾⌐ denotes a ligature in the source.

J.M.